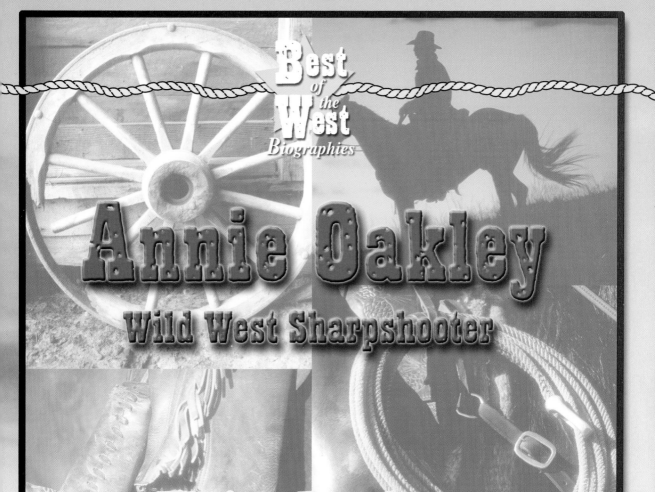

Best of the West Biographies

Annie Oakley
Wild West Sharpshooter

Elaine Landau

Enslow Publishers, Inc.

40 Industrial Road   PO Box 38
Box 398   Aldershot
Berkeley Heights, NJ 07922 Hants GU12 6BP
USA   UK
http://www.enslow.com

To Sarah Sutin

Library of Congress Cataloging-in-Publication Data

Landau, Elaine.
     Annie Oakley : wild west sharpshooter / Elaine Landau.
        p. cm. — (Best of the West biographies)
     Summary: Introduces the life of Phoebe Ann Moses, later known as Annie Oakley, who began shooting game after her father's death to feed her family and became the star sharpshooter of Buffalo Bill's Wild West show.
     Includes bibliographical references and index.
     ISBN 0-7660-2205-6 (hardcover : alk. paper)
     1. Oakley, Annie, 1860-1926—Juvenile literature.
2. Shooters of firearms—United States—Biography—Juvenile literature. 3. Entertainers—United States—Biography—Juvenile literature. [1. Oakley, Annie, 1860-1926.
2. Sharpshooters. 3. Entertainers. 4. Women—Biography.]
I. Title. II. Series.
GV1157.O3L36 2004
799.3'092—dc21
                           2003001944

Printed in the United States of America

10 9 8 7 6 5 4 3 2 1

To Our Readers: We have done our best to make sure that all Internet Addresses in this book were active and appropriate when we went to press. However, the author and publisher have no control over and assume no liability for the material available on those Internet sites or on other Web sites they may link to. Any comments or suggestions can be sent by e-mail to comments@enslow.com or to the address on the back cover.

Photo Credits: © Corel Corporation, pp. i, ii–iii, 5, 8, 11, 14, 21, 25, 34, 41 (background), 42–48 (background); © Denver Public Library, pp. 6, 19, 28, 29, 35; Associated Press, pp. 27, 40; Buffalo Bill Historical Center (Cody, Wyoming), pp. 7, 22, 30; Photos.com, p. 23; The Darke County Historical Society, Inc., pp. 6, 9, 13, 15, 26, 32, 36, 37, 41 (inset); The Ohio Historical Society, pp. 16, 18, 20.

Cover Photo: © Denver Public Library

Contents

Annie Oakley was one of the stars
of *Buffalo Bill's Wild West.*

Ladies and Gentlemen . . . Miss Annie Oakley!

It was a wonderful night. *Buffalo Bill's Wild West* was in town. People had waited weeks for the show. Now every seat was filled. The audience was anxious to see the show's star.

Bugles sounded. There was a drum roll. The ringmaster stepped forward. He yelled to the crowd, "Ladies and Gentlemen, Miss Annie Oakley, the little girl of the Western Plains!"

Seconds later, a horse galloped forward. Its rider was a short, slender female. She wore a fringed buckskin dress and a broad-brimmed hat. The young woman was holding a large rifle. Smiling, she waved to the crowd. They were there to see her. She would not disappoint them.

Annie Oakley always amazed the crowd when she made her shots from a horse—without slowing down.

A cowboy rode just ahead of her. He tossed small glass balls into the air. These did not stay up long. Without slowing her horse's pace, the young woman aimed her rifle. She fired at the balls, hitting them all. Broken glass fell like rain. The crowd burst into applause.

That was just the start of her act. She had many amazing shots. The young woman might shoot the cork off a bottle. Then, she would shoot the flame off a candle. Seeing her was always worth the price of a ticket. She was Annie Oakley, the sharpshooter known as "Little Sure Shot."

Annie Oakley did what few other women

could do. This slim young woman stood just five feet tall. Yet she could handle a rifle better than most men. She became famous all over the world. Annie Oakley appeared before royalty. She won many medals. She left audiences everywhere dazzled.

But Annie Oakley was much more than just a Wild West star. She was also an unusually determined and hard-working person. She often used her shooting skills to help others. This is a book about Annie Oakley—the woman who picked up a gun for all the right reasons.

One of Annie Oakley's most famous trick shots was aiming at her targets in a mirror. She would shoot them without ever turning around.

Annie's Early Days

People think they know a lot about Annie Oakley. But how much of what they know really happened? Annie Oakley was a Wild West star. However, she was not from the West. Her real name was not Annie Oakley, either. It was Phoebe Ann Moses. This is her true story.

Phoebe Ann Moses was born on a farm in Woodland, Ohio, on August 13, 1860. Susan and Jacob Moses were Annie's parents. They had come to Ohio from Pennsylvania to farm. The couple had heard about the region's rich, fertile soil. They settled there hoping to do well.

Back then, Ohio was different from the way it is today. Then, the area was thick with forests. Annie's family used some of those trees to build a cabin.

At the time, most farm families were large. Many people were needed to work the land and do the chores. There were eight children—seven girls and a boy—in the Moses family. However, one of the girls died. So Annie grew up with five sisters and a brother. Her older sisters always called her Annie. They thought the name Phoebe Ann was too long and fancy.

Annie was a pretty child. She had thick, wavy brown hair. Her blue-gray eyes sparkled when she laughed. Yet in many ways, Annie was not what people expected in a little girl. She was active, high spirited, and loved the outdoors. Annie felt happiest in the woods surrounding their

Annie's mother, Susan Moses, worked hard on their family farm.

cabin. She was naturally curious and enjoyed exploring their land.

But the Moses children did not have much time for play. The family was very poor. Annie and the others spent most of the day working alongside their parents.

Annie's sisters usually helped their mother. They cooked and did laundry. The girls planted a garden for extra food. They also canned the fruits and vegetables grown on the farm.

Annie preferred to work outdoors with her father. She helped plant and harvest crops. Annie fed and cared for the farm animals. Her father taught her to use cornstalks to make traps. They caught rabbits, quails, and squirrels in these. These animals were food for the Moses family.

Life for Annie's family was never easy. But things got even worse in the winter of 1866. The trouble began on a cold winter morning. Jacob Moses had hitched up the wagon and left the farm early that day. He wanted to bring some corn and wheat to the mill. On the way home, he planned to pick up supplies.

In the 1800s, people traveled in wagons pulled by horses.

The trip was not usually a difficult one. But that day the weather changed without warning. By early afternoon it was already snowing heavily. A blizzard had started and Jacob Moses was caught in it.

Annie's family worried as the hours passed. Mr. Moses should have been home before dark. But hours later, there was still no sign of him.

Finally, he arrived home just after midnight. It was an unsettling sight. Jacob Moses had nearly frozen to death. His hands were curled into tight fists, and he had been unable to hold the reins. Somehow, the horses had found their way back in the storm.

Jacob Moses never fully recovered. Annie's family tried to nurse him back to health. But he died that spring. Annie was just five-and-a-half years old at the time.

The death of Annie's father took its toll on the family. Mrs. Moses had to sell the farm. The Moses family rented a smaller piece of property. Annie's mother also had to go out to work. She became a nurse. She worked long hours but never made very much money.

Although Annie was young, she tried to help. She set more traps to catch animals. Annie also had her eye on the rifle that hung above the fireplace. It had belonged to her father. She knew that she could bring in even more meat with a gun. But Mrs. Moses had warned the children not to touch the rifle.

The Moses family were Quakers. They were against violence. Annie's mother felt that there was no place in their lives for guns. Yet Annie did not want the gun to hurt others. She wanted to use it to help her family.

One day while her mother was out, Annie took down the gun. Then, she went into the woods to look for game. She returned that evening with meat for dinner. After that, Mrs. Moses allowed Annie to hunt. No one had ever taught her to shoot. The eight-year-old was a natural. She usually hit her targets with a single shot.

Although no one ever taught Annie how to shoot, she was naturally talented at handling a gun.

Growing Up

In 1867, Annie's mother remarried. At first, it looked as if things might improve. It did not turn out that way, though. Annie's mother had another baby. Soon after that, her new husband was killed in an accident. Annie's mother was on her own again. Only now, there was another mouth to feed.

The family needed help. To ease things, some of the children went to live with neighbors. In 1870, Annie moved in with Nancy Ann and Samuel Edington. The Edingtons ran the Darke County Infirmary in nearby Greenville. People with special needs lived at the infirmary. These included orphans and the

homeless. People with serious mental problems lived there, too.

Annie helped Mrs. Edington. She sewed clothes at the Infirmary. Annie learned to knit and use a sewing machine. She even took up fancy embroidery. Annie sent the extra money she earned to her mother.

Annie was not at the Infirmary long. A local

Annie and her family lived in this house after their mother remarried, but they did not stay there long.

farmer wanted her to live with his family. His wife needed help with their new baby. The farmer promised to send Annie's pay to her mother. He also said that Annie could go to school. There was to be time for her to hunt as well.

Annie agreed to go with him. That was a mistake. The farmer had lied about everything.

Annie was made to work from four o'clock in the morning until well after dark. She was treated

The Darke County Infirmary was in Greenville, Ohio.

like a prisoner and was not allowed to leave.
Both the husband and wife beat her.

After two years, Annie finally ran away. She
returned to the Infirmary. The farmer came
looking for her there. He wanted to take Annie
back. But the Edingtons would not permit it.
They had seen her scars from his beatings.
Instead, Annie remained with the Edingtons.
They taught her to read and write. They also
paid Annie for her sewing. The Edingtons
treated her like a daughter.

Nevertheless, Annie never forgot how cruel
the farm family had been. She called them
"wolf" people, after the tale of the wolf in
sheep's clothing. The farmer had seemed nice at
first, but had become mean. Annie had thought
about running away from the "wolves" sooner.
She only stayed because she knew her mother
needed the money. Yet as it turned out, the
"wolves" never gave Annie's mother a cent.

Annie returned home when she was about
fifteen. Her mother had married for a third
time. Annie hunted almost every day. She

brought in enough game to keep the family well-fed. Annie sold the extra meat to a nearby grocer. He, in turn, sold the meat to fancy hotels. Some were as far away as Cincinnati. That was about eighty miles from where Annie lived.

Annie's older sister, Lydia, had married and moved near Cincinnati. When Annie visited her in 1875, she saw some of those hotels. One

invited her to take part in a special shooting match just outside the city. To win, Annie had to hit more targets than the other person in the match, a handsome man in his twenties named Frank Butler.

Frank Butler fell in love with Annie when he saw her shoot.

Butler would not be easy to beat. He made his living as a sharpshooter.

Nevertheless, Annie wanted to try. The prize was fifty dollars. The money would mean a lot to her family. During the match, Frank Butler and Annie took turns shooting live pigeons. They shot the birds as they were released from their traps. At first, the match was tied. But then Butler missed his last shot. That made Annie the winner.

Annie made every shot in the contest.

Annie was thrilled to have won. Frank Butler was thrilled to have met Annie. Butler saw that Annie was special. Few young women had her skill and spunk. While Annie was at her sister's house, Frank Butler saw a lot of her. Their feelings for one another grew stronger.

Frank Butler owned a large white poodle named George. George did not like many people. Yet he took to Annie. Frank Butler knew that Annie was right for him. Annie felt the same way about Frank Butler.

Annie often said that the couple married on August 23, 1876, when Annie was just sixteen. However, the marriage certificate was dated 1881. In any case, at the time of her wedding, Annie had no idea how exciting her life was about to become.

George, the poodle, liked Annie right away.

A Star Is Born!

Annie had married a sharpshooter. Frank Butler had a shooting partner he worked with on stage. But one May evening in 1882, his partner became ill and could not do the show. So, Butler asked Annie to help.

Butler wanted Annie to hold up his targets. But she had other ideas. She wanted to shoot on stage. Frank Butler gave in and never regretted it.

Annie missed her first target that night. Some people think she did this on purpose. After that, the audience grew tense. They wanted to see what this small girl with a big gun could do. When Annie succeeded on her next try, the crowd went wild. They clapped,

Annie Oakley rarely missed her target.

whistled, and stomped their feet. One thing was
clear. Annie had a future in show business.

Annie became Frank Butler's new partner.
She used the stage name Annie Oakley. No
one is certain why Annie chose that name.
Oakley may have been the name of an Ohio
town she liked.

Frank Butler and Annie Oakley spent a lot of time on the road. They performed in cities throughout the Midwest. The poodle, George, was always with them. George was even part of the act. Either Oakley or Butler would shoot an apple off the dog's head. After the show, George took a bow with them.

Annie Oakley did many other tricks, as well. Sometimes she shot the ashes off Frank Butler's cigarette. Other times, she shot coins he held up. Before long, everyone knew about their act. Annie Oakley had many fans.

The famous Sioux chief, Sitting Bull, was one of her fans. Sitting Bull had seen Annie Oakley perform. The two became friends

Sitting Bull was a famous medicine man and leader of the Sioux.

after they met in 1884. Oakley reminded Sitting Bull of his daughter who had died. He gave Annie Oakley a special American Indian name. It meant "Little Sure Shot" in English. People would call her that for years.

Frank Butler and Annie Oakley were pleased with their success. But life on the road was not easy. Oakley worked on new stunts for hours. She also sewed all her own costumes. The sewing skills she learned at the Infirmary came in handy now.

Some towns they went to held shooting matches. Oakley took part in these before her evening shows. It was a way to earn the extra cash she needed. Annie Oakley still sent money home. She never forgot her family.

Buffalo Bill's Wild West

Annie Oakley and Frank Butler worked in many different places. Sometimes they traveled with circuses. They also did shooting stunts in comedy skits. After a while, only Oakley performed. Butler felt that she was the real star. He became her business manager. Butler helped Oakley think of new stunts, too.

By the 1880s, Annie Oakley had learned to do more than shoot. She had also become an outstanding horsewoman. Oakley loved doing daring stunts on horseback. The crowds enjoyed these, as well.

But Annie Oakley really became famous after joining *Buffalo Bill's Wild West* in 1885. *Buffalo Bill's Wild West* was an exciting show. It gave people a taste of America's frontier days. Cowboys in the show rode bucking broncos and roped calves. American Indians also performed. They played traditional songs on their drums and did dances that had special meanings. Sometimes, the cowboys and American Indians pretended to have battles.

But audiences liked Annie Oakley's act

In addition to being an expert sharpshooter, Annie Oakley was also a talented horseback rider.

best. She was the show's star. Oakley's stunts were amazing. Sometimes she would jump over a table and grab a gun. Then, she would shoot an object that had been tossed into the air. Annie Oakley always hit her mark before it touched the ground.

Colonel William F. Cody, better known as "Buffalo Bill," was a famous frontiersman and sharpshooter.

In another stunt, a small, silver disk was the target. Oakley never looked directly at it. Instead, she would turn around and see the disk in a mirror. With her rifle on her shoulder, Annie Oakley would shoot the disk out of a cowboy's hand.

Buffalo Bill's Wild West performers traveled a great deal. The show played in many cities across the country. Annie Oakley was a hit wherever she went. But she was especially popular in New York.

The performers in *Buffalo Bill's Wild West* were popular everywhere they went.

There, fans waited in line to meet her. Many people came to see her perform. Women wearing evening gowns and jewels clapped as Oakley hit her targets. The Ladies' Riding Club of New York honored Annie Oakley. The members awarded her a gold medal. It was just one of many medals she received.

Annie Oakley enjoyed being famous. But

Buffalo Bill led a parade down the streets of New York to advertise for the show.

she never forgot what it was like to be poor. She often tried to help people who were less fortunate. While in New York, Oakley invited children from an orphanage to the show. She paid for their tickets. She also bought them popcorn and ice cream. Annie Oakley made it a day they would never forget.

Annie Oakley was not just famous in the United States. She became a star in Europe, as well. It all started in 1887 when *Buffalo Bill's Wild West* went to England. The show was there to help celebrate Queen Victoria's Golden Jubilee. The jubilee marked the queen's fifty years on the throne.

Distinguished Visitors to Buffalo Bill's Wild West. London. 1887.

Many important people in Europe attended *Buffalo Bill's Wild West*. Queen Victoria, top center, was one of them.

Queen Victoria enjoyed Annie Oakley's act. Thousands of other people there did, as well. Oakley was invited to all the best restaurants and parties. Fashion designers copied Annie Oakley's costumes. Women in London started dressing like her.

A number of men also wrote to Annie Oakley. They asked her to marry them. They did not know that Oakley was already married. She was called "Miss Annie Oakley" in the show. Annie had never met most of these men. But they had seen the show and claimed to love her.

Annie Oakley received gifts and flowers from her English fans. She gave most of the flowers to nearby hospitals. Oakley also helped some charities in England. She frequently took part in shooting matches. Annie Oakley gave her prize money to groups that helped women and children. She continued to send money home to her own family, as well.

After England, *Buffalo Bill's Wild West* went to other European countries. But Annie

Oakley and Frank Butler did not go with the show. For a while, Oakley performed on her own. She and Butler went to Germany. There, Annie Oakley did a special show for the Crown Prince.

She and Butler also worked alone in New York for a time. Oakley did shooting matches. She did some acting, too. Annie Oakley starred in another Wild West show, as well.

But in 1889, Annie Oakley went back to *Buffalo Bill's Wild West*. The show was about to begin another tour of Europe. Their first stop was Paris, France. The show also played in Belgium, Germany, Holland, and England. As always, Oakley delighted audiences everywhere.

Annie Oakley received many medals for her skills with her gun.

People wrote books and magazine articles about Annie Oakley. All kinds of stories about her arose. The girl from Ohio was becoming a legend. Some people said that Oakley had once captured an outlaw gang. Others swore that she was an American Indian fighter. Still another story had Annie shooting a grizzly bear when she was only five.

None of this was true. But for years, many people thought it was. The truth was that Annie Oakley was a highly skilled performer. She spent many hours practicing, performing, and making costumes. She also always rode in *Buffalo Bill's Wild West* parades. The parades were usually held quite early in the morning. Oakley was often tired, but she still took part.

While on the road, Annie Oakley and Frank Butler stayed in a tent. Yet Oakley tried to make it feel like home. She had a rug, folding furniture, and a bathtub. She even made curtains for the door opening. Later, Oakley would often look back fondly on those days. She wrote, "The travel and early parades were hard, but I was happy."

6

The Later Years

In the fall of 1892, *Buffalo Bill's Wild West* returned to the United States. The show had been in Europe for over three years. Annie Oakley and Frank Butler were glad to be back. They bought some vacant land in Nutley, New Jersey. Oakley designed a house, and they built it together. It was the first house of their own.

Annie Oakley was still with *Buffalo Bill's Wild West*. From March to October, she and Butler traveled with the show. During the rest of the year, Oakley took on other projects. Once she went to London, England to star in a play. It was the story of a female sharpshooter!

By now, Annie had done quite a bit of traveling. But her life was about to change. On

October 29, 1901, she was in a train wreck. Oakley was traveling with *Buffalo Bill's Wild West* when it happened. Over a hundred of the show's horses were killed in the crash. Stories differ about Oakley's injuries. But it is certain that she then decided to leave the show for good.

Frank Butler worked for a company that made ammunition. As a former sharpshooter, he knew a lot about guns. Annie Oakley did

Annie Oakley and Frank Butler had been married for seventeen years before they finally had a real house of their own.

shooting exhibitions. She also did more acting. A play called *The Western Girl* was written just for her.

People liked to think of Annie Oakley as being young. This was true even as she grew older. When she performed, she was still called the "young Annie Oakley" or the "Western girl." Through the years, Oakley had stayed slim and quick-moving. However, she could not stop her

Annie Oakley starred in *The Western Girl* in 1902.

THE GREAT CLIFF SCENE.
NANCE BARRY SAVES LIEUT. HAWLEY.

hair from turning
white. So for a while
she wore a brown wig.
Everyone thought she
was much younger
than she was. In 1911,
Oakley joined up with
another traveling Wild
West show. She was
fifty-one years old at
the time. But Annie
Oakley did not stay
long. She was ready for
a more relaxing life.

Even when she was older, people liked to think of Annie Oakley as a free-spirited young woman.

She and Frank Butler sold
their New Jersey home. Now
they would only spend summers
in the north. The couple stayed in hotels in
Florida and North Carolina during the winter.
Oakley was not ready to completely stop
working. She still gave shooting exhibitions.

Annie Oakley also gave shooting lessons.
She wanted more women to be able to learn

to protect themselves. Often, she taught groups of girls and women for free.

In 1917, American soldiers went to fight in World War I. Annie Oakley wrote to the War Department. She offered to train a division of women soldiers. These women could protect the home front while the men went off to war. The government did not take her idea. But Annie Oakley was actually ahead of her time. Today, women serve as both soldiers and police officers.

Annie Oakley often gave shooting lessons for free.

Oakley tried to be helpful in other ways, as well. Two of her sisters had died of the lung disease tuberculosis. Annie Oakley visited tuberculosis patients in hospitals. She raised money for their treatment, too.

But on November 9, 1922, Annie Oakley was in a serious car accident. She survived, but suffered from a broken hip and ankle. She spent the next six weeks in the hospital. Frank Butler visited her there every day. She received thousands of cards and letters from fans. People had not forgotten her.

In time, Annie Oakley's health improved. During the next three years, she continued her shooting exhibitions. She began to write her own life story, too. Unfortunately, the book was never finished. In 1925, Oakley learned that she had a serious blood disorder. She grew weaker over the next year. Annie Oakley died on November 3, 1926. The famous female sharpshooter was sixty-six years old at the time.

Frank Butler had also been ill. He died just eighteen days after she did. The couple had been married for fifty years.

Annie Oakley was gone, but her memory lived on. Still more books and plays were written about her. Later on, there were movies, TV shows, and even Annie Oakley comic books.

When people thought of women from the Wild West, many thought of Annie Oakley.

But Annie Oakley's story is important for another reason. It shows that with enough effort, nearly anything is possible. Oakley went from being poor to being a star. It was not easy. Her success came from hard work and years of practice. In many ways, Annie Oakley's life was about overcoming odds.

Annie Oakley's rule for getting ahead was simple. She once said, "Aim at a high mark and you'll hit it. No, not the first time. . . . But keep on aiming . . . for practice will make you perfect. Finally, you'll hit the bull's eye of success."

The members of the Annie Oakley Women's Shooting Association still honor her by decorating her grave with flowers and flags.

Dave, the All-American Dog. . . . Woof!

After leaving *Buffalo Bill's Wild West*, Annie Oakley and Frank Butler got a new dog. The dog's name was Dave. Dave hunted and fished with them. He was like a member of the family.

Dave also helped the country. During the first World War, Dave raised money for charity. The dog had his own shows. In them, people would hide money in handkerchiefs. Dave always sniffed out the hiding places. All the money Dave found went to the Red Cross, a relief organization that aids people during war or disasters.

Dave became well known. Annie Oakley and Frank Butler even sent out holiday cards from

their special pet. The cards read: *"Christmas Greetings From Dave."*

Timeline

1860—Phoebe Ann (Annie) Moses is born on August 13.

1866—Jacob Moses, Annie's father, dies.

1867—Annie's mother marries her second husband.

1870—Annie goes to live with Nancy Ann and Samuel Edington.

1875—Annie meets Frank Butler.

1876 or 1881—Annie and Frank Butler marry on August 23.

1882—Annie adopts the stage name "Annie Oakley" and performs with her husband as a sharpshooter for the first time.

1884—Annie Oakley meets and becomes friends with Chief Sitting Bull.

1885—Annie Oakley joins *Buffalo Bill's Wild West*.

1887—Annie Oakley goes to England with *Buffalo Bill's Wild West* to celebrate Queen Victoria's Golden Jubilee.

1889—Annie Oakley goes to France and other countries with *Buffalo Bill's Wild West*.

1892—Annie Oakley returns home and builds a house in New Jersey.

1901—Annie Oakley is in a train wreck on October 29. She leaves *Buffalo Bill's Wild West* after the accident.

1917—The United States enters the first World War. Annie Oakley offers to train a division of women soldiers.

1922—Annie Oakley is injured in an automobile accident on November 9.

1926—Annie Oakley dies on November 3 at the age of sixty-three.

Words to Know

bronco—A small, wild horse.

buckskin—A strong, soft material made from the skins of deer or sheep.

bugle—A musical instrument that is shaped like a trumpet.

comedy skit—A short, funny play.

embroidery—A picture or design sewn on with thread.

fertile—Able to grow crops or produce fruit.

frontier—The far edge of a country where few people live.

hitched—Fastened, usually with rope.

jubilee—A large celebration to mark the anniversary of a special event.

legend—A story or tale handed down through the years.

orphan—A child whose parents are dead.

pioneer—One of the first people to explore or settle in a new area.

Quakers—People who are members of a Christian religion. Quakers stress peace and reject war.

sharpshooter—An expert shooter who can hit difficult targets.

Sioux—A memeber of a group of American Indian tribes that of the North American plains.

stunt—An act that takes some skill or daring.

target—An object to shoot at.

Reading About Annie Oakley

Alter, Judy. *Wild West Shows: Rough Riders and Sure Shots*. Danbury, Conn.: Franklin Watts, 1997.

Dadey, Debbie. *Shooting Star: Annie Oakley, the Legend*. New York: Walker, 1999.

Hicks, Peter. *You Wouldn't Want To Live In a Wild West Town!* Danbury, Conn.: Franklin Watts, 2002.

Krensky, Stephen. *Shooting for the Moon: The Amazing Life and Times of Annie Oakley*. New York: Farrar, Straus & Giroux, 2001.

Macy, Sue. *Bull's-Eye. A Photobiography of Annie Oakley*. Washington, D.C.: National Geographic, 2001.

Ruffin, Frances E. *Annie Oakley*. New York: Powerkids Press, 2002.

Shields, Charles J. *Annie Oakley*. Broomall, Penn.: Chelsea House, 2001.

Internet Addresses

Women In History: Annie Oakley

An outstanding Web site containing lots of information about Annie Oakley. There are wonderful photos here, too.

<http://www.lkwdpl.org/wihohio/
oakl-ann.htm>

Annie Oakley—A Dorchester Library Profile

An interesting Web site on Annie Oakley's rise to fame.

<http://www.dorchesterlibrary.org/library/
oakley.html>

Women of the West Online

Web site of a museum that explores the ongoing roles of women in shaping the American West.

<http://www.autry-museum.org/explore/
exhibits/wwmonline>

Index